A LOOK AT EARTH'S ROCKS

WHAT ARE MINERALS?

BY KRISTEN RAJCZAK NELSON

Gareth Stevens PUBLISHING

CRASHCOURSE

Please visit our website, www.garethstevens.com. For a free color catalog of all our high-quality books, call toll free 1-800-542-2595 or fax 1-877-542-2596.

Cataloging-in-Publication Data
Names: Rajczak Nelson, Kristen.
Title: What are minerals? / Kristen Rajczak Nelson.
Description: New York : Gareth Stevens Publishing, 2018. | Series: A look at earth's rocks | Includes index.
Identifiers: ISBN 9781482462463 (pbk.) | ISBN 9781482462456 (6 pack) | ISBN 9781482462449 (library bound)
Subjects: LCSH: Minerals--Juvenile literature.
Classification: LCC QE365.2 R285 2018 | DDC 549--dc23

First Edition

Published in 2018 by
Gareth Stevens Publishing
111 East 14th Street, Suite 349
New York, NY 10003

Designer: Samantha DeMartin
Editor: Kristen Nelson

Photo credits: Series background winnond/Shutterstock.com; caption box Edhar Shvets/Shutterstock.com; cover, p. 1 De Agostini/R. Appiani/Getty Images; p. 5 (turquoise) Jiri Vaclavek/Shutterstock.com; p. 5 (mica, halite) Branko Jovanovic/Shutterstock.com; p. 5 (pyrite) Cagla Acikgoz/Shutterstock.com; p. 5 (quartz) Albert Russ/Shutterstock.com; p. 7 Vadim Petrakov/Shutterstock.com; p. 9 ronenr/Getty Images; p. 11 (main) Peter Hermes Furian/Shutterstock.com; p. 11 (inset) Dorling Kindersley/Getty Images; p. 13 Joel Arem/Getty Images; pp. 15, 17 (top) Pi-Lens/Shutterstock.com; p. 17 (bottom) MrBright/Shutterstock.com; p. 19 (gold) optimarc/Shutterstock.com; p. 19 (nickel) Sementer/Shutterstock.com; p. 21 Charles D Winters/Getty Images; p. 23 Wally Eberhart/Getty Images; p. 25 Ahmad Rashdan/Shutterstock.com; p. 27 YolLusZam1802/Shutterstock.com; p. 29 (bottom) D Winters Charles/Getty Images; p. 29 (top) Mettus/Shutterstock.com; p. 30 (all) MarcelClemens/Shutterstock.com.

Printed in the United States of America

CPSIA compliance information: Batch #CS17GS: For further information contact Gareth Stevens, New York, New York at 1-800-542-2595.

CONTENTS

Words in the glossary appear in **bold** type the first time they are used in the text.

MINERAL MAKEUP

Minerals have been forming for billions of years. To be called a mineral, matter must be an **inorganic** solid that occurs naturally and have a certain makeup, or composition. This composition must be the same everywhere the mineral is found.

QUARTZ

MICA

TURQUOISE

HALITE

PYRITE

MAKE THE GRADE

A mineral is a homogenous solid, which means its **chemical** composition is the same throughout. Its **properties** won't change if you cut it in half!

HOW THEY FORM

Minerals are the matter in the ground that forms rocks. When **magma** rises and cools, minerals are left in the cracks of rock. Minerals may also be the result of wind and water wearing down rock, settling, and hardening in new forms.

MAKE THE GRADE

All rocks are made up of one or more minerals.

Some minerals **dissolve** in water and can be carried to a new place. When the water **evaporates**, the minerals re-form. Finally, minerals can form from other minerals when conditions around them change, such as a rise in heat.

SALT CRYSTALS LEFT BEHIND IN THE DEAD SEA

MAKE THE GRADE

Rocks commonly have the grains, or very small parts, of several minerals mixed together, so it can be hard to see them individually.

MAIN MINERAL FEATURES
SET CHEMICAL COMPOSITION
INORGANIC
NATURALLY OCCURRING
SOLID
GROW CRYSTALS

GLOSSARY

chemical: having to do with matter that can be mixed with other matter to cause changes

dissolve: to mix completely into a liquid

element: matter that is pure and has no other type of matter in it

evaporate: to change from a liquid to a gas

identify: to find out the name or features of something

inorganic: being made of matter other than plant and animal

jewelry: pieces of metal, often holding gems, worn on the body

luster: the glow of light off an object rubbed smooth

magma: hot, liquid rock inside Earth

pattern: the way colors or shapes happen over and over again

property: something used to tell a member of a group or one individual from another

structure: the way something is arranged, or set up

FOR MORE INFORMATION

BOOKS

Brannon, Cecelia H. *A Look at Minerals*. New York, NY: Enslow Publishing, 2016.

DK Publishing. *Rocks and Minerals: Facts at Your Fingertips*. New York, NY: DK Publishing, 2012.

WEBSITES

Photo Gallery: Minerals
science.nationalgeographic.com/science/photos/minerals/
See pictures and read about many kinds of minerals found on Earth.

Publisher's note to educators and parents: Our editors have carefully reviewed these websites to ensure that they are suitable for students. Many websites change frequently, however, and we cannot guarantee that a site's future contents will continue to meet our high standards of quality and educational value. Be advised that students should be closely supervised whenever they access the Internet.

INDEX